Robert E. Lee

Character and Valor

Robert E. Lee

Character
and
Valor

Compiled and Edited by

Rod Gragg

PELICAN PUBLISHING COMPANY
Gretna 2010

Copyright © 2001
By Rod Gragg
All rights reserved

First published by Rutledge Hill Press as *A Commitment to Valor: A Character Portrait of Robert E. Lee*, 2001
Published by arrangement by Pelican Publishing Company, Inc., 2010

First edition, 2001
First Pelican edition, 2010

> *The word "Pelican" and the depiction of a pelican are trademarks
> of Pelican Publishing Company, Inc., and are registered in the
> U.S. Patent and Trademark Office.*

Library of Congress Cataloging-in-Publication Data

Robert E. Lee : character and valor / compiled and edited by Rod Gragg.
    p. cm.
    Includes bibliographical references (p.).
    ISBN 978-1-58980-7655
    1. Lee, Robert E. (Robert Edward), 1807-1870. 2. Lee, Robert E. (Robert Edward), 1807-1870—Military leadership. 3. Lee, Robert E. (Robert Edward), 1807-1870—Quotations. 4. Conduct of life—Quotations, maxims, etc. 5. United States—History—Civil War, 1861-1865—Quotations, maxims, etc. 6. Generals—Confederate States of America—Biography. I. Gragg, Rod.

E467.1.L4 C658 2001
973.7'3'092—dc21
                                                                                00-068853
                                                                                CIP

All the photographs in this book are courtesy of the National Archives.

Jacket design: Gore Studio Inc.

Printed in the United States of America
Published by Pelican Publishing Company, Inc.
1000 Burmaster Street, Gretna, Louisiana 70053

For Matt and Skip

Contents

Preface	9
Ackowledgments	11
Robert E. Lee Biography	13
1. Duty	17
2. Leadership	27
3. Integrity	39
4. Dignity	49
5. Kindness	57
6. Responsibility	67
7. Courage	79
8. Self-Control	89
9. Humility	101
10. Faith	111
Lee's Letter to Gen. Winfield Scott	121
Lee's Orders for the Invasion of Pennsylvania	123
Lee's Order for Worship	125
Lee's Farewell Address	127
Notes	129

Preface

Upon completing his definitive four-volume study of Robert E. Lee, historian Douglas Southall Freeman—who would earn a Pulitzer Prize for *R. E. Lee, A Biography*—recalled the multitude of challenges he had encountered in producing the monumental work. Yet, he proclaimed, "I have been fully repaid by being privileged to live, as it were, for more than a decade in the company of a great gentleman."

Modern critics and revisionist historians have criticized Robert E. Lee for siding with Virginia and the South, and have sometimes accused him of various failures: failing to employ defensive tactics at Gettysburg, focusing too much on the defense of Richmond, failing to reprimand or motivate subordinates, declining command of Federal forces in the war's opening days and other retrospective condemnations. Despite revisionist criticism of Lee, however, countless students of the American Civil War continue to share Douglas Southall Freeman's opinion of the general.

Amid the vastly different lifestyles of modern American society, literate Americans who discover anew the life of Robert E. Lee are often affected with the same awe and admiration as Lee's contemporaries. Despite the best efforts of the most jaded revisionists and the harshest critics, generation after generation of Americans and others have encountered the Lee of history and, as have so many before them, find themselves marveling at the character and conduct of Robert E. Lee.

Today, Lee remains the embodiment of all that was good and noble in the Old South. Despite the passage of time and the ever-changing whims of

★ PREFACE ★

popular culture, he has remained America's most admired military leader. This is not a work of history or biography, although history and biography are treated seriously and, I hope, faithfully in this book. It is a collection of observations by and about Lee that focuses on the caliber of character that has made Robert E. Lee an American hero for the ages.

Acknowledgments

I have been blessed to have been so exposed to the heart of this exceptional American, and I am grateful to those who helped me with this work. Special thanks go to Paul Fowler, a librarian at Coastal Carolina University's Kimbel Library. His research skills and broad knowledge of the Civil War were invaluable to this project. Larry Stone, the president of Rutledge Hill Press, offered valuable direction in the formation of this work. My editor, Geoff Stone, was both thoroughly professional and consistently pleasant despite deadline pressures. I'm also grateful to Debbie Shaub for her able assistance, and to my mother, Elizabeth Gragg, whose cheerful spirit and Southern cooking were priceless. Deep love and thanks also go to my family: especially my wife Cindy, and all my children: Skip, Matt, Penny, Joni, Elizabeth, Rachel and Faith. I am most indebted—like Lee—to the promise of John 3:16.

Rod Gragg
Conway, South Carolina

Robert E. Lee Biography

Robert E. Lee was a Virginian. The third son of Henry "Light-Horse Harry" Lee and Ann Hill Carter, Lee was born at Stratford in Westmoreland County, Virginia on January 19, 1807. His father, who died when Lee was eleven, distinguished himself as a cavalry commander in the Continental army during the American Revolution, served in the U.S. Congress and the Virginia legislature, and was also governor of Virginia—all before Lee's birth.

Financial hardship forced Lee's family to leave Stratford and move to Alexandria, Virginia, when Lee was a boy. He was appointed to the U.S. Military Academy at West Point, and graduated second in the class of 1829 without a demerit. Two years later, he married Mary Ann Custis, the great-granddaughter of Martha Washington. She was a member of a distinguished Virginia family and lived at Arlington, which overlooked the Potomac River opposite Washington, D.C. The Lees enjoyed almost forty years of marriage and raised seven children: three sons—George Washington Custis, William H. Fitzhugh, and Robert Edward—and four daughters—Mary, Agnes, Annie, and Mildred.

As an officer in the Army Corps of Engineers, he directed military engineering projects along the South's Atlantic coast, on the Mississippi, and in New York City's harbor. During the Mexican War, he served with distinction as a captain on the staff of Gen. Winfield Scott, and was cited for valor for crucial reconnaissance missions. After the war he was placed in command of constructing Fort Carroll in Baltimore's harbor. From 1852–1855, he served as superintendent at West Point, where he made important improvements to the curriculum. He was promoted to lieutenant-colonel of the 2nd U.S. Cavalry and served on the Texas frontier, but was forced to return home to Arlington when his father-in-law died and chronic arthritis left his wife an invalid. While in Virginia in 1859, he was ordered to Harper's Ferry when John Brown and his raiders seized the U.S. arsenal, and directed the assault that captured Brown and ended the takeover. In February 1860 he took command of the U.S. Army's Department of Texas with the rank colonel. He remained at that post until recalled to Washington on the eve of war in 1861.

Although he opposed secession and considered slavery "a moral and political evil," Lee felt his primary allegiance lay with Virginia. He declined field command of U.S. forces when Virginia moved to secede and resigned from the army. He accepted command of Virginia's military forces with the rank of general. After holding command in western Virginia and directing the coastal defenses of South Carolina and Georgia, he was recalled to Richmond as military advisor to Pres. Jefferson Davis. When Gen. Joseph E. Johnston, commander of the Confederate army defending Richmond, was wounded at the battle of Seven Pines on May 31, 1862, Lee replaced him. In the Seven Days Campaign, Lee repulsed the Federal Army of the Potomac under Gen. George B. McClellan. He routed Gen. John Pope at Second Manassas in August of 1862, but his follow-up invasion of the North was checked by McClellan at the battle of Antietam several weeks later. He decisively defeated Gen. Ambrose E. Burnside at Fredericksburg in December, and shattered Gen. Joseph Hooker's offensive at Chancellorsville in May of 1863. His masterful command of the Army of Northern Virginia kept the Confederacy alive.

Lee's second attempt to take the war to the North failed in a disastrous defeat at Gettysburg on July 1–3, 1863, but he managed to save his army on the retreat back to Virginia. He withstood furious assaults by the Army of the Potomac under Gen. Ulysses S. Grant at the Wilderness, Spotsylvania and Cold Harbor, and was promoted to general-in-chief of all Confederate armies in early 1865. His depleted army could not maintain its defensive line at Petersburg, however, and he was forced to abandon Richmond and make the retreat that ended in his surrender at Appomattox, Virginia, on April 9, 1865.

After the war, he moved to Lexington, Virginia, to assume the presidency of Washington College (which later became Washington and Lee University). In his postwar years, he did much to encourage reconciliation between North and South. He remained president of the college until his death at Lexington on October 12, 1870, at age 63. After attending a church leaders' meeting in Lexington one chilly afternoon in late September 1870, Lee walked home in a cold rain to join his wife and daughters for supper. As he stood to say grace, he was stricken by what appears to have been a stroke. Two weeks later, on October 12, 1870, he died at age sixty-three.

In 1975, the United States Congress restored Robert E. Lee's U.S. citizenship. Today he is acclaimed as one of history's greatest military commanders, and is renowned for the strength of his character.

Chapter 1

DUTY

Robert E. Lee's lasting legacy was his devotion to duty—a character trait he learned at an early age. His father, "Light-Horse Harry" Lee, lost the family fortune when Lee was a child, then spent five years trying to regain his wealth only to die unsuccessful and separated from his family. Young Robert E. Lee was left to restore the family name, and he succeeded by doing his duty.

At West Point, he distinguished himself in scholarship and military expertise—and graduated without a demerit. His most difficult decision—determining whether to remain in the U.S. Army or side with the South when Virginia seceded—was finally resolved when he concluded that his first duty lay with his state. "When his course was once decided upon," noted a wartime observer, "he never faltered, and never for a moment regretted his decision, or doubted that he was treading the path of duty."[1]

★ DUTY ★

$\mathcal{D}$uty . . . is the sublimest word in our language. Do your duty in all things. . . . You cannot do more—you should never wish to do less.[2]

—*Lee, in a prewar letter to his son*

★ ★ ★

$\mathcal{P}$rivate and public life are subject to the same rules; and truth and manliness are two qualities that will carry you through this world much better than *policy*, or *tact* or *expediency*, or any other word that was ever devised to conceal or mystify a deviation from a straight line.[3]

—*From a note found in Lee's dispatch case after his death*

★ DUTY ★

I cannot raise my hand against my birthplace, my home, my children.[4]
> —*Lee, on why he accepted command in the Southern army*

★ ★ ★

From the first commencement of our troubles he had decided that in the event of Virginia's secession, duty . . . would compel him to follow.[5]
> —*Lee's wife, Mary, recalling her husband's priority of duty*

★ **DUTY** ★

Virginia is my country, her I will obey, however lamentable the fate to which it may subject me.[6]

—*Lee, anticipating Virginia's secession*

★ ★ ★

General Lee ... showed a personal disinterestedness, and an unselfish devotion to principles and country, rarely to be met with in this world.[7]

—*Confederate Vice President Alexander Stephens*

I did only what my duty demanded; I could have taken no other course without dishonor."[8]

Arlington, Washington City P.O., April 20, 1861

Hon. Simon Cameron, Secretary of War,

Sir: I have the honor to tender my resignation of my command as colonel of the First Regiment of Cavalry.

>Very respectfully your obedient servant,
>R. E. Lee, Colonel First Cavalry[9]

—Lee's 1861 letter resigning his commission in the U.S. Army, written upon his conclusion that his first duty was to Virginia

★ **DUTY** ★

$\mathcal{I}$ plan and work with all my might to bring the troops to the right place at the right time; with that I have done my duty.[10]

—*Lee, responding to a foreign military observer's inquiry about strategy*

★ ★ ★

$\mathcal{I}$ cannot see a single ray of pleasure during this war; but as long as I can perform any service to the country, I am content.[11]

—*From a wartime letter by Lee to his wife*

★ ★ ★

$\mathcal{H}$ow easily I could get rid of this and be at rest. I have only to ride along the lines, and all will be over. But it is our duty to live.[12]

—*Lee, to a staff officer, as he prepared to surrender at Appomattox*

In the session of 1866–67, when Washington and Lee University was crowded with students, General Lee being its President, a young man opened my door and invited me to his room. I saw that he had been weeping, and [he explained that he had been called] to General Lee's office.

The General called attention to his very low grade in Latin, then took the different studies, all of which grades were very low. . . . Finally, he called the young gentleman's attention to the very large number of unexcused class absences, and [he] admitted that he had not attended his recitations as he should have done.

His confession seemed to make General Lee very sad indeed, and he sat in silent thought for some time. He then said that if he mailed the report to [the student's] parents it would give them great pain. . . . General Lee sat for some time in deep thought, and then gently he began to tear the report into strips one by one. [The student] broke down entirely and wept. As soon as he became quiet, General Lee said to him, "Son, we cannot undo the past; that is forever gone; but the future is in our hands . . ." He said to me that he rose to his feet and extended his hand to General Lee, saying, "General, I will do it." I am sure that General Lee was never again made sad by one of his reports.[13]

—Anecdote recalled by a postwar alumnus of Washington College

★ DUTY ★

I cannot desert my native state in the hour of her adversity. I must abide by her fortunes, and share her fate.[14]

> —*Response by Lee in 1865 to an English nobleman's offer to escape the destruction of postwar Virginia*

★ ★ ★

*A*s a general principle, you should not force young men to do their duty, but let them do it voluntarily and thereby develop their characters. . . . Make no needless rules.[15]

> —*Lee to faculty members while president of Washington College*

★ **DUTY** ★

$\mathcal{Y}$ou must expect discomforts and annoyances all through life. No place or position is secure from them, and you must make up your mind to meet with them and bear them.[16]

—From a letter by Lee to his daughter, Agnes

★ ★ ★

So consistent was [Lee's] life, so devoted to duty, without a glance to right or left, so fixed on the golden rule.[17]

—An officer who served under Lee, delivering a eulogy upon his death

Chapter 2

LEADERSHIP

Robert E. Lee knew how to exercise authority in a manner which inspired and motivated those under his command. He set high standards, but was not arrogant. He encouraged, but he did not flatter. He reproved subordinates when necessary, but he did not embarrass or demean those who failed. He avoided excessive familiarity with his officers and men, but demonstrated a consistent personal interest in them. He formed his battle plans carefully, then issued orders decisively. He chose his key subordinates selectively, then delegated broad authority to them. Their exceptional respect and affection for him was a measure of his leadership. In the anguish of Appomattox, one battle-hardened Johnny Reb may have spoken for all when he yelled from the defeated ranks, "I love you just as much as ever, General Lee."[1]

★ **LEADERSHIP** ★

So great is my confidence in General Lee that I am willing to follow him blindfolded.[2]

—*Stonewall Jackson, speaking of Lee*

★ ★ ★

*T*here were never such men in an army before. They will go anywhere and do anything if properly led.[3]

—*Lee, commenting on his troops in 1863*

★ ★ ★

It was remarkable what confidence the men reposed in General Lee; they were ready to follow him wherever he might lead, or order them to go.[4]

—*A private in the Army of Northern Virginia*

Success is not always attained by a single undivided effort, [and] it rarely follows a halting vacillating course. [5]

★ **LEADERSHIP** ★

$\mathcal{I}$ am content to share the rations of my men.[6]
—*Lee, declining a luxurious gift of delicacies*

★ ★ ★

The men hung around him and seemed satisfied to lay their hands on his gray horse or to touch the bridle, or the stirrup, or the old general's leg—anything that Lee had was sacred to us fellows.[7]
—*A veteran, recalling soldiers' reactions as Lee rode through the ranks*

★ ★ ★

He always invited [other] views . . . not so much for the purpose of having his own views approved and confirmed as to get new light; . . . [he] was more pleased when he found something that gave him new strength than with efforts to evade his questions by compliments.[8]
—*Gen. James Longstreet, remembering Lee's willingness to receive suggestions from subordinates*

★ **LEADERSHIP** ★

Before [Lee took command], the Rebel troops were sickly, half fed and clothed, and had no hearts for their work. [Afterwards], the troops improved in appearance. Cadaverous looks became rare among prisoners. The discipline became better; they went into battles with shouts and without being urged, and, when in, fought like tigers. . . . A more marked change for the better never was made in any body of men than that wrought in his army by the sensible actions of General Lee.[9]

—A Northern newspaper reporter who covered the war in Virginia in 1862

★ ★ ★

When his course was decided upon, he never faltered, and never for a moment regretted his decision, or doubted that he was treading the path of duty.[10]

—A wartime observer of Lee's command style

★ **LEADERSHIP** ★

History will hold Lee to be a great soldier, wise in counsel, patient in preparation, swift in decision, terrible in onset, tenacious of hold, [and] sullen in retreat.[11]

—Capt. John Hampden Chamberlayne,
13th Virginia Light Artillery Battalion

★ ★ ★

His name might be Audacity. He will take more desperate chances, and take them quicker than any other general in this country, North or South.[12]

—Col. Joseph Ives, an officer who served on Lee's staff

★ **LEADERSHIP** ★

His soldiers reverenced him and had unbounded confidence in him, for he shared all their privations.[13]

—*A Southern officer, recalling Lee's natural leadership abilities*

★ ★ ★

I must now leave the matter to your reflection and good judgment. Make up your mind what is best to be done under all the circumstances which surround us, and let me hear the result at which you arrive.[14]

—*Lee to Stonewall Jackson on the eve of battle*

★ LEADERSHIP ★

Next morning a small group of horsemen appeared. . . . It became known that General Lee was amongst them, and a crowd gathered along the way, silent and bare-headed. There was no excitement—no cheering. Yet as the great chief passed, a deep loving murmur . . . rose from the very hearts of the crowd.[15]

—A wartime observer, recalling the response of Southerners in contact with Lee

★ ★ ★

He knows what he is about.[16]

—Southern diarist Mary Boykin Chesnut

★ **LEADERSHIP** ★

The popularity of Lee in the South . . . is the consequence of the unbounded confidence of the soldiers in Lee. They know him to be brave, have seen him tried, and think that all goes well while he remains to conduct matters. He is said never to lose spirit, and inspires the same confidence in others. His kindness of manner to his men has increased this confidence. He takes care of his men, and is very particular in his attention to their wants on the march. He would not suffer them to be hurried without necessity, gives them sufficient opportunities for rest and refreshment, and would inquire among them at the end of the day how they had stood the march. When the march is necessarily a hard one it is his custom to send back couriers, when the point aimed at is near at hand, to encourage his weary men with this intelligence. His men are said to love to record these stories of his devotion to them.[17]

—From an analysis of Lee's leadership by the New York Herald *in January of 1865*

It is particularly incumbent on those charged with instruction of the young to set them an example.[18]

—Lee, commenting on the basis of leadership

★ ★ ★

One of the best ways that I know of to induce the students to attend chapel is to be sure we attend ourselves.[19]

—Lee, to faculty as president of Washington College

★ ★ ★

When a man makes a mistake, I call him to my tent, talk to him, and use the authority of my position to make him do the right thing the next time.[20]

—Lee, advising a subordinate officer on discipline

★ **LEADERSHIP** ★

The self-denial, the stainless manhood, the unfaltering faith in the saving truths of the Bible, the enormous willpower—submissive as a child to God's will—the roundness and completeness of such a life, should be a model and an inspiration to the young men of our whole country.[21]

*—A Southern officer who served with
Lee for the duration of the war*

★ ★ ★

As Lee came riding alone into Richmond [after his surrender], his old followers immediately recognized him. They formed in line and followed him to his home where, with uncovered heads, they saw him enter his door. Then they silently dispersed.[22]

—Pvt. John H. Worsham, 21st Virginia Infantry

Chapter 3

INTEGRITY

When they chanced to encounter their former commander after the war, some Southern veterans would remove their hats and stand respectfully at attention in silent salute. Children who had the opportunity to shake Lee's hand would still marvel decades later at the memory of the meeting. Such was the power of Lee's presence. Few public figures in any age have bequeathed such an enduring legacy of national respect and affection, and seldom has any military commander so effused his troops with the love and admiration displayed toward Lee by his soldiers. The esteem in which Robert E. Lee has been held by generations is due not just to the competency of his command, but also to the quality of his character.[1]

★ **INTEGRITY** ★

I knew there was no use to urge him to do anything against his ideas of what was right.[2]
—*Gen. Ulysses S. Grant, recalling a conversation with Lee after his surrender*

★ ★ ★

He was a foe without hate, a friend without treachery, a soldier without cruelty, and a victim without murmuring. He was a public officer without vices, a private citizen without wrong, a neighbor without reproach, a Christian without hypocrisy, and a man without guile.[3]
—*A Southern political leader, contemplating Lee's death*

. . . if you are virtuous and laborious you will accomplish all the good you propose to yourself.[4]

★ INTEGRITY ★

At the close of the war, offers of pecuniary assistance poured in upon [Lee] from all quarters, but he steadfastly refused to receive them. . . . Soon after he went to Lexington [to assume the presidency of Washington College], he was visited by an agent of a certain insurance company, who offered him their presidency, at a salary of *ten thousand dollars* per annum; he was then receiving only *three thousand* from the college. He told the agent that he could not give up the position he then held, and could not properly attend to the duties of both.

"But, general," said the agent, "we do not want you to discharge any duties. We simply wish the use of your name; *that* will abundantly compensate us.

"Excuse me, sir," was the prompt and decided rejoinder. "I cannot consent to receive pay for services I do not render."[5]

—*The Rev. William J. Jones, chaplain, 13th Virginia Infantry*

★ INTEGRITY ★

If you will act in accordance with the dictates of your conscience, to the best of your judgment . . . you will do right.[6]

—Lee, responding to an inquiry for political advice

★ ★ ★

In this enlightened age, there are few I believe, but what will acknowledge that slavery as an institution is a moral and political evil in any country.[7]

—From a letter by Lee in 1860

★ ★ ★

If the slaves of the South were mine, I would surrender them all without a struggle to avert the war.[8]

—Lee, speaking on the eve of war

★ **INTEGRITY** ★

So far from engaging in a war to perpetuate slavery, I am rejoiced that slavery is abolished. . . . I would cheerfully have lost all I have lost by the war and suffered all I have suffered, to have this object attained.[9]

—*Lee, commenting on slavery after the war*

★ ★ ★

It is to men of . . . high integrity and commanding intellect that the country must look to give character to her councils, that she may be respected and honored by all nations.[10]

—*Reflection by Lee upon the death of a respected colleague*

★ ★ ★

Say just what you mean to do on every occasion, and take it for granted you mean to do right.[11]

—*Lee, from a letter to his son Custis*

★ **INTEGRITY** ★

$\mathcal{T}$he general commanding is pained to learn that the vice of gambling exists, and is becoming common in this army. . . . He regards it as wholly inconsistent with the character of a Southern soldier and subversive of good order and discipline in the army. All officers are earnestly enjoined to use every effort to suppress this vice, and the assistance of every soldier having the true interests of the army and of the country at heart is invoked to put an end to a practice which cannot fail to produce those deplorable results which have ever attended its indulgence in any society.[12]

—Lee's General Order Number 127, issued to the Army of Northern Virginia in 1862

★ ★ ★

$\mathcal{W}$hile I wish to do what is right, I am unwilling to do what is wrong.[15]

—From a letter by Lee to his son Custis in 1860

★ **INTEGRITY** ★

𝒜pproved, and respectfully returned to Captain _____, with the advice that he should always respect the religious views and feelings of others.[13]

—Order by Lee allowing a Jewish soldier to attend Synagogue over the objections of his captain

★ ★ ★

𝐼 hope you may be as firm in your principles as I am in mine.[14]

—Lee, to a Pennsylvania woman who declared her support for the North

★ **INTEGRITY** ★

He possessed every virtue of the other great commanders without their vices.[16]
—*From a eulogy to Lee by U.S. Sen. Benjamin Hill*

★ ★ ★

I think it is better to do right, even if we suffer in so doing, than to incur the reproach of our consciences and posterity.[17]
—*Lee, advising against revenge in 1864*

★ **INTEGRITY** ★

He not only possessed true genius . . . but he had what was better than genius—a heart whose every throb was in harmony with the teachings of the Great Captain whom he served.[18]

—*Gen. John B. Gordon, CSA*

Chapter 4

DIGNITY

Even amid the coarseness of wartime, Robert E. Lee projected a natural dignity. He was not aloof; those who knew him praised him for his personal warmth. His manner, however, was distinctively reserved. He did not appear pompous or self-righteous; he simply projected a sense of dignity that seemed to promote a high standard of conduct from those in his company. "His presence," observed a contemporary, "possessed that grave and simple majesty which commanded instant reverence and repressed familiarity; and yet so charmed by a certain modesty and gracious deference, that reverence and confidence were ever ready to kindle into affection. It was impossible to look upon him and not to recognize at a glance . . . a man created great and good."[1]

★ **DIGNITY** ★

Oh, I wish he was ours!²

*—A Maryland Unionist who viewed Lee
as he passed her home in 1862*

★ ★ ★

General Lee had a quiet dignity which forbade all undue familiarity . . . but in the social circle there was about him a charming affability and courtesy which won the hearts of all who had the privilege of meeting him thus.³

—A wartime friend of Lee's

★ ★ ★

I am General Lee, and I am most happy to have met you.⁴

*—Lee, to a farmer who engaged him in a long
conversation then asked to meet Robert E. Lee*

He was always and everywhere the refined gentleman.[5]

★ **DIGNITY** ★

I was standing in the door of our headquarters in Richmond about the middle of April, 1861, when my attention was attracted by a man approaching; he wore a uniform. It was not the uniform that attracted my attention but the man himself. He was tall and straight, and I thought the handsomest specimen of manhood I had ever seen, both in face and figure. He made such an impression that as he came opposite me I could not keep from looking at him, and when he had passed my eyes followed him, until I actually stepped outside of the door in order to keep him in sight. . . . I followed and asked some friend who that splendid looking man was. He informed me that it was Colonel Robert E. Lee.[6]

—*Pvt. John H. Worsham, 21st Virginia Infantry*

★ **DIGNITY** ★

A soldier would have as soon thought of kissing the lips of a raging volcano as of telling a coarse jest in his presence.[7]
—*A Southern veteran*

★ ★ ★

Even in the fleeting moment of his passing by my gate, I was awed by his incomparable dignity.[8]
—*A Virginia homeowner who viewed the passing of Lee's army*

★ ★ ★

In manner, [Lee was] grave and dignified . . . which gave him the air of a man who kept up his pride to the last.[9]
—*A Northern officer, observing Lee at Appomattox*

★ DIGNITY ★

General Lee is, almost without exception, the handsomest man of his age I ever saw. He is fifty-six years old, tall, broad-shouldered, very well made, well set up—a thorough soldier in appearance; and his manners are most courteous and full of dignity. . . . I imagine no man has so few enemies, or is so universally esteemed. Throughout the South, all agree in pronouncing him to be as near perfection as a man can be. He has none of the small vices, such as smoking, drinking, or swearing, and his bitterest enemy never accused him of any of the greater ones.

He generally wears a well-worn long gray jacket, a high black felt hat, and blue trousers tucked into his Wellington boots. I never saw him carry arms, and the only mark of his military rank are the three stars on his collar. He himself is very neat in his dress and person, and in the most arduous marches he always looks smart and clean.[10]

—Lt. Col. Arthur Fremantle, a British military observer, en route to Gettysburg

★ **DIGNITY** ★

Scrupulously neat in his dress, he was always simply attired, and carefully avoided the gold-lace and feathers in which others delighted.[11]

—An acquaintance of Lee, recalling his dignified attire

★ ★ ★

His majestic composure, his rectitude and his sorrow were so wrought and blended into his visage and [were] so beautiful and impressive.[12]

—A Confederate veteran, recalling Lee's army on the march

★ ★ ★

All the force which personal appearance could add . . . was imparted by his manly form, and the great dignity as well as grace in his every action and movement.[13]

—A Southern political leader, recalling his first impression of Lee as commander

★ DIGNITY ★

General Lee was . . . the very personification of dignity and grace and I can never forget the impression he made on us all.[14]

—Pvt. George F. Peterkin, 21st Virginia Infantry

★ ★ ★

He is a perfect gentleman in every respect.[15]

—Lt. Col. Arthur Fremantle's diary for 1863

Chapter 5

KINDNESS

As the Army of Northern Virginia marched northward during the Gettysburg Campaign, a sweat-soaked private broke from the ranks and approached General Lee. "Please General," the man said, "I came aside to this old hill to get a rag or something to wipe the sweat out of my eyes." Lee promptly handed his personal handkerchief to the soldier. It was a typical act of kindness for Lee. On another occasion, an exhausted courier fell asleep in Lee's tent—on the general's cot. Lee covered him with a blanket and left him to rest undisturbed. Such kindnesses endeared him to his troops—as demonstrated by the battled-hardened veteran who encountered Lee while walking to the rear with a shattered arm. "I grieve for you, my poor fellow," Lee told him. "Can I do anything for you?" Replied the wounded soldier: "Yes sir, you can shake hands with me, General, if you will consent to take my left hand."[1]

★ **KINDNESS** ★

He was so gentle, kind and almost motherly in his bearing.[2]

—*A student at Washington College during Lee's tenure as president*

★ ★ ★

A child thrown among a knot of strangers would inevitably be drawn to him . . . and would run to claim his protection.[3]

—*A London Times reporter who observed Lee in wartime*

Occupy yourself in helping those more helpless than yourself.[4]

★ **KINDNESS** ★

How can you say so, General? Now, I wish that they were all at home attending to their own business, and leaving us to do the same.[5]

—Lee, responding to an officer who had wished aloud that all the enemy were dead

★ ★ ★

I have fought against the people of the North because I believed they were seeking to wrest from the South dearest rights. But I have never cherished toward them bitter or vindictive feelings, and have never seen the day when I did not pray for them.[6]

—Lee, to a friend who condemned the North at war's end

★ **KINDNESS** ★

One day in the autumn of 1869, I saw General Lee standing at his gate, talking to a humbly-clad man, who turned off . . . just as I came up. After exchanging salutations, the general pleasantly said, pointing to the retreating form, "That is one of our old soldiers who is in necessitous circumstances." I took it for granted that it was some veteran Confederate, and asked to what command he belonged, when the General politely and pleasantly added, "He fought on the other side, but we must not remember that against him now."

The man afterward came to my house and said to me, in speaking of his interview with General Lee: "Sir, he . . . not only had a kind word for an old soldier who fought against him, but he gave me some money to help me on my way." What a beautiful illustration of the teaching . . . "If thine enemy hunger, feed him; if he thirst, give him drink."[7]

—*A neighbor of Lee's in Lexington, Virginia*

★ KINDNESS ★

The prisoners that we have here, General _____, are my prisoners; they are not General Grant's prisoners, and as long as I have any rations at all I shall divide them with my prisoners.[8]

—Lee, responding to a proposal that Northern prisoners receive less food in retaliation for destruction caused by General Grant's troops

★ ★ ★

My man, go back to your quarters, and never let it be said you were found asleep on your post.[9]

—Order by Lee dismissing charges against an exhausted sentry accused of sleeping on duty

★ ★ ★

Young man, you should have some feeling for your horse, dismount and rest him.[10]

—Lee, reproving a youthful courier for neglecting his winded mount

★ KINDNESS ★

We were marching to Maryland, and our division was resting in the shade on an unused old road. Many of our "boys" were prone upon this road, with knapsacks under our heads, resting, when we noticed the approach of four or five officers on horses. As they dew near we recognized Gen. A. P. Hill, General Lee and two or three staff officers. General Hill was a few feet in advance, and, as he drew near he said, "Move out of the road, men." Immediately General Lee said, "Never mind, General; we will ride around them. Lie still, men." As he spoke he turned his horse to the left, and General Hill was equally as quick to pull out of the road. They passed within twenty feet of me. Did I see General Hill's face flush, or did I imagine it? I do not think General Lee thought of rebuking General Hill, then or ever. It was just his way, his consideration for others, especially his soldiers.[11]

—Pvt. Theodore Hartman, 14th Tennessee Infantry

★ KINDNESS ★

Treat the whole field alike.[12]
> —*Lee's orders to hospital attendants, directing the same medical treatment for wounded troops whether Southern or Northern*

★ ★ ★

So, young ladies, if the music is good, go and hear it as often as you can, and enjoy yourselves.[13]
> —*Lee, to a group of young ladies criticized for attending a concert of "Yankee band music" while their town was occupied by Northern forces*

★ KINDNESS ★

$\mathcal{I}$ cannot help that he is a good soldier and would be useful in a higher position.[14]

—Lee, defending his decision to endorse a promotion for an officer who had once denounced him

★ ★ ★

In the rush of this age, a character so simply meek and so proudly, grandly strong is scarce comprehensible.[15]

—An elderly Confederate veteran, reflecting on Lee in the early twentieth century

★ KINDNESS ★

Howdy do, my man.[16]
> —Lee, responding to a "feeble-minded" soldier who ignored military protocol and greeted him with "Howdy do, dad"

★ ★ ★

His tenderness to his children, especially his daughters, was mingled with a delicate courtesy which belonged to an older day than ours, a courtesy which recalls . . . knightly times.[17]
> —A friend of Mrs. Lee, remembering visits to the general's home

Chapter 6

RESPONSIBILITY

Robert E. Lee was a model of responsibility. Personally and professionally, he was dependable and punctual. As a commander, he demonstrated responsibility by his careful preparation and his decisive execution. When his army was successful, he gave the credit to the Lord and to his troops. When the army failed, he blamed only himself. At Appomattox, he assumed responsibility for surrendering his army in person. When urged to evade surrender by waging guerrilla warfare, he chose instead to act responsibly and end the war with honor. Robert E. Lee began his command and completed it by setting an example of responsibility faithfully assumed and executed.[1]

★ **RESPONSIBILITY** ★

Combined with valor, fortitude and boldness, . . . it should lead us to success.[2]

—Lee, endorsing a responsible attitude toward hard work

★ ★ ★

He did not shrink from the grave responsibilities and arduous labors which he knew must be encountered.[3]

—A longtime associate, recalling Lee's attitude toward command

★ ★ ★

I think it very strange, lieutenant, that an officer of this command, which has been here a week, should come to me, who am just arrived, and ask who is his ordnance officer and where to find his ammunition.[4]

—Lee, newly in command, reproving a subordinate for irresponsibility

... upon my shoulders rests the blame.[5]

★ **RESPONSIBILITY** ★

General Lee asked one of his [generals] who was riding with him if a work he had ordered to be performed was finished. The officer replied, hesitatingly, that it was. Lee then proposed to ride to the spot and inspect it. On arriving there he found that the work had made little progress . . . Lee rode quietly on.
While doing so he began to compliment his companion on the fine charger he rode.

"Yes sir," replied the general, "he is a splendid animal, and I prize him the more highly because he belongs to my wife and is her favorite riding horse."

"A magnificent horse indeed," was General Lee's reply, "but I should not think him safe . . . for a lady, and I would urge you by all means to take some of the mettle out of him before you suffer your wife to ride him again. *And, by the way, general, I would suggest to you that the rough paths along these trenches would be admirable ground over which to tame him.*"

It need scarcely be said that the rebuked officer did not trust the reports of subordinates from that time forward.[6]

—*Brig. Gen. A. L., II Corps Chief of Artillery, Army of Northern Virginia*

★ RESPONSIBILITY ★

I consulted with him with confidence, and adopted his suggestions with entire assurance.[7]

—Gen. Daniel E. Twiggs, commending
Lee during the Mexican War

★ ★ ★

Mildness and forbearance, tempered by firmness and judgment, will strengthen their affection for you, while it will maintain your control over them.[8]

—Lee, at age thirty-two, to his wife Mary on
the subject of responsible child-rearing

★ **RESPONSIBILITY** ★

Never do a wrong thing to make a friend or keep one; the man who requires you to do so is dearly purchased at a sacrifice.[9]
> —*From a letter by Lee to his son, noting the responsibilities of friendship*

★ ★ ★

Such conduct is unauthorized and discredible.[10]
> —*Lee, stating his intent to punish Southern troops accused of plundering*

★ **RESPONSIBILITY** ★

Soon afterwards I joined General Lee, who was engaged in rallying and in encouraging the broken troops [from Pickett's charge at Gettysburg]. His face, which is always placid and cheerful, did not show signs of the slightest disappointment, care, or annoyance; and he was addressing to every soldier he met a few words of encouragement, such as, "All this will come right in the end . . . but in the meantime, all good men must rally. We want all good and true just now. . . .

I saw General Wilcox (an officer who wears a short round jacket and a battered straw hat) come up to him, and explain, almost crying, the state of his brigade. General Lee immediately shook hands with him and said cheerfully, "Never mind, General, all this has been my fault—it is I that have lost this fight, and you must help me out of it in the best way you can.[11]

—*Lt. Col. Arthur Fremantle, who witnessed Lee's reaction to the failure of Pickett's Charge*

★ RESPONSIBILITY ★

We must never make a rule that we cannot enforce.[12]
—*Lee, commenting on the responsibilities of discipline*

★ ★ ★

It has also been reported that some men in this army have been so unmindful of their obligations to their comrades, and of their own characters, as to engage in the occupation of purchasing supplies of food and other things, for the purpose of selling them at exorbitant prices to their fellow soldiers. . . . A just regard for the reputation of the army requires the immediate suppression of this great evil.[13]

—*An 1862 order by Lee outlawing price-gouging in the Army of Northern Virginia*

★ **RESPONSIBILITY** ★

Yes, I know they will say hard things of us; they will not understand how we were overwhelmed by numbers; but that is not the question, colonel; the question is, is it right to surrender this army? If it is right, then *I* will take *all* the responsibility.[14]

—Lee, assuming responsibility for surrendering his army despite potential condemnation

★ ★ ★

We must all, however, resolve on one thing—not to abandon our country.[15]

—Lee after Appomattox, dismissing suggestions that he should flee the country

★ RESPONSIBILITY ★

Responsibilities that clearly belonged to him as a soldier he met promptly and to the fullest extent.[16]

—A fellow officer, recalling Lee's response to the challenges of command

★ ★ ★

Try not to even wish for what you ought not to have, but try hard to be truly good.[17]

—From a letter by Lee to his eleven-year-old daughter

★ **RESPONSIBILITY** ★

All that is bright must fade, and we ourselved have to die. Keep this in view and live to that end.[18]

*—Lee, urging responsible conduct in a
prewar letter to one of his children*

★ ★ ★

We make a great deal of our own happiness and misery in this world, and we can do more for ourselves than others can do for us.[19]

*—Lee to his daughter Agnes, commending
the virtue of personal responsibility*

Chapter 7

COURAGE

Robert E. Lee repeatedly demonstrated fortitude under fire. A quieter, less obvious valor marked the entire course of his life. He demonstrated consistent courage as a boy by tending to a mother who was chronically ill, and by faithfully caring for an invalid wife for much of his adult life. When he turned down Federal field command in 1861, he exercised the courage of his convictions by siding with family, home, and state. His courageous command decisions made him the model for generations of American military professionals. He also had the courage to surrender his depleted army when further fighting would only have produced useless loss of life. Throughout his life, he exhibited fortitude toward faith, family and duty. Robert E. Lee was a courageous man.[1]

⋆ **COURAGE** ⋆

Let danger never turn you aside from the pursuit of honor or the service of your country.[2]

—Lee, addressing the issue of personal conduct in warfare

★ ★ ★

This officer, greatly distinguished at the siege of Vera Cruz, was again indefatigable during these operations, in reconnaissance as daring as laborious, and of the utmost value. Nor was he less conspicuous in planting batteries, and in conducting columns to their stations under the heavy fire of the enemy.[3]

—Citation by Gen. Winfield Scott, honoring Lee during the Mexican War

You must study to be frank with the world: frankness is the child of honesty and courage.[4]

I declined the offer . . . to take command of the army that was to be brought into the field, stating as candidly and as courteously as I could that, though opposed to secession and deprecating war, I could take no part in the invasion of the Southern states.[5]

—Lee, on why he turned down field command of Northern forces in 1861

★ ★ ★

Lee was the most aggressive man I met in the war, and was always ready for an enterprise.[6]

—Maj. John S. Mosby, commander, Mosby's Rangers

★ COURAGE ★

The Texans cheered lustily as their line of battle . . . swept across our artillery pit and its adjacent breastwork. Much moved by the greeting of these brave men and their magnificent behavior, General Lee spurred his horse through an opening in the trenches and followed close on their line as it moved rapidly forward. The men did not perceive that he was going with them until he had advanced some distance in the charge. When they did, there came from the entire line, as it rushed on, the cry, "Go back, General Lee! Go back! We won't go on until you go back!" A sergeant seized his bridle rein.[7]

—Col. Charles S. Venable, describing Lee's attempt to accompany his troops into combat at the battle of the Wilderness

★ COURAGE ★

General Lee mounted and rode a few paces to my right and . . . while there a shell burst immediately in front of old Traveler, who reared up and stood as straight as I ever saw a man. The General sat serene until the horse came down on his two fore feet.[8]

—*Pvt. J. B. Minor, 1st Richmond Howitzers*

★ ★ ★

The blow, whenever struck, must, to be successful, be sudden and heavy.[9]

—*Lee, endorsing bold action as central to the art of war*

★ **COURAGE** ★

I found him with our twenty-gun battery, looking as calm and dignified as ever, and perfectly regardless of the shells bursting round him and the solid shot plowing up the ground in all directions.[10]

—A Confederate officer, describing Lee's demeanor under fire

★ ★ ★

Tell her I can only think of her and pray for her recovery. I wish I could be with her to nurse her and care for her.[11]

—Lee, writing to one of his daughters in 1864, inquiring about his invalid wife, Mary

★ COURAGE ★

It is argued that Lee was strong only in defense, and was averse to taking the offensive. Nothing could be more false. . . . Witness the bold transfer of his army from Richmond to the Rapidan, while McClellan's troops still rested on the James River. Witness the audacity of detaching Jackson from the Rappahannock line to seize Manassas Junction and the road to Washington in Pope's rear. . . . Witness that crowning glory of his audacity, the change of front to attack Hooker, and that march around what Hooker called "the best position in America, held by the finest army on the planet." Witness his invasion of Pennsylvania, a campaign whose only fault was the generous fault of over-confidence in an army whose great deeds might, if anything, excuse it—an over-confidence, as we ourselves know, felt by every man he led, and which made us reckless of all difficulties, ready to think that to us nothing was impossible. He was a commander who had met no equal.[12]

—*Maj. Walter H. Taylor, Lee's adjutant-general*

★ **COURAGE** ★

Lee was an aggressive general, a fighter. To succeed, he knew battles were to be won, and battles cost blood. . . . Although always considerate and sparing of his soldiers, he would pour out their blood when necessary.[13]

*—Gen. G. Moxley Sorrell, brigade commander,
Army of Northern Virginia*

★ ★ ★

I pray we may not be overwhelmed. I shall, however, endeavor to do my duty and fight to the last."[14]

*—Letter from Lee on 22 February 1865, approximately
six weeks before Appomattox*

★ **COURAGE** ★

General, you and I as Christian men have no right to consider only how this would affect us. We must consider its effect on the country as a whole. Already it is demoralized by four years of war. If I took your advice, the men would be without rations and under no control of officers. They would be compelled to rob and steal in order to live . . . We would bring on a state of affairs it would take the country years to recover from.[15]

 —*Lee at Appomattox, responding to Gen. Edward Porter Alexander's proposal that the South wage guerrilla warfare instead of surrendering*

★ ★ ★

Then there is nothing left me to do but to go and see General Grant, and I would rather die a thousand deaths.[16]

 —*Lee at Appomattox, concluding that he must surrender his army*

Chapter 8

SELF-CONTROL

Lee governed his life through self-discipline. Throughout his life he practiced self-denial. It was not unusual for an officer to keep a stock of fine liquor; Lee's beverage of choice was chilled buttermilk. Many officers dined well in the field; Lee chose soldier's rations. Some commanders surrounded themselves with the trappings of power. Lee dressed modestly and exercised command with a small, well-selected staff. He chose his words and his associates with care, and his actions reflected the wisdom borne of discipline. Few leaders have faced such challenges as confronted Robert E. Lee during the War Between the States. Yet, he mastered most situations—perhaps because he had first learned to master himself.[1]

★ SELF-CONTROL ★

I cannot consent to place in the control of others one who cannot control himself.[2]

—*Lee, commenting on the importance of self-control to command*

★ ★ ★

Students looking for an example . . . will find in the life of Lee an inspiration to noble living and high endeavor such as is nowhere else found. . . . [He was] a man whose strength was the might of gentleness and self-command.[3]

—*Excerpted from a eulogy to Lee by one of his contemporaries*

We must not . . . yield to difficulties, but strive the harder to overcome them.[4]

★ **SELF-CONTROL** ★

$\mathcal{D}$esire nothing too eagerly, nor think that all things can be perfectly accomplished according to our own notions.[5]

*—Lee, in a letter to his wife during
his prewar service in Texas*

★ ★ ★

He was exceedingly abstemious in his own habits. He never used tobacco, and rarely took even a single glass of wine. Whiskey or brandy he did not drink, and he did all in his power to discourage their use by others.[6]

—J. William Jones, chaplain, Army of Northern Virginia

★ **SELF-CONTROL** ★

Upon another occasion General Lee proposed to "treat" some of his officers, remarking, " I have just received a demijohn which I know is *of the best*." The demijohn, tightly corked, was produced, drinking-vessels were brought out, and all gathered around in eager expectancy, when the general filled the glasses and cups to the brim—not with old "Cognac" or "Bourbon"—but with *fresh buttermilk*, which a kind lady, knowing his taste, had sent him. He seemed to enjoy greatly the evident disappointment of some of the company when they ascertained the true character of their "treat."[7]

*—Recollection of a headquarters "drinking bout"
by a member of Lee's command*

★ **SELF-CONTROL** ★

Tell all the boys to get their hoes and go to the corn fields. Labor is the thing to make soldiers. They will then be able to do their share when they become men.[8]

—From a letter by Lee to his brother Carter in 1863

★ ★ ★

If you have a fault to find with anyone, tell him, not others. . . . There is no more dangerous experiment than that of undertaking to be one thing before a man's face and another behind his back.[9]

—Admonishment to exercise self-control from a family letter by Lee

★ SELF-CONTROL ★

It is important that conflict not be provoked before we are ready.[10]
>—Lee, stating the importance of discipline
>to command decision-making

★ ★ ★

Ah, General Hood, when you Texans come about, the chickens have to roost mighty high.[11]
>—Lee to Gen. John Bell Hood, encouraging him to
>restrain his Texas troops from appropriating local
>fowl and livestock to supplement rations

★ SELF-CONTROL ★

Scarcely less to be admired than his sublime devotion to duty was his remarkable self-control. General Lee was naturally of a positive temperament, and of strong passions; but he held these in complete subjection to his will and conscience. He was not one of those invariably amiable men whose temper is never ruffled; but when we consider the immense burden which rested upon him, and the numberless causes for annoyance with which he had to contend, the occasional cropping out of temper which we, who were near him, witnessed, only showed how great was his habitual self-control.

He had a great dislike for reviewing army communications. . . . On one occasion when [doing paperwork], he manifested his ill-humor by a little nervous twist or jerk of the neck and head, peculiar to himself, accompanied by some harshness of manner. I petulantly threw the paper down at my side and gave evident signs of anger. Then, in a perfectly calm and measured tone of voice, he said, "Colonel Taylor, when I lose my temper, don't you let it make you angry."[12]

—*Maj. Walter H. Taylor, Lee's adjutant-general*

★ **SELF-CONTROL** ★

You would not have your general run away and hide. He must stay and meet his fate.[13]
>—*Lee, responding to end-of-war suggestions that he flee possible arrest*

★ ★ ★

It should be the object of all to avoid controversy, to allay passion, give full scope to reason and every kind feeling."[14]
>—*From a letter by Lee to Virginia's governor, advising self-control in times of tension*

★ ★ ★

The statement is not true; but I have not thought proper to publish a contradiction, being unwilling to be drawn into a newspaper discussion, believing that those who know me would not credit it, and those who do not would care nothing about it.[15]
>—*Lee, replying to entreaties that he respond to an untrue attack by a Northern newspaper during Reconstruction*

★ SELF-CONTROL ★

$\mathcal{I}$ look forward to better days, and trust that time and experience, the great teachers of men, under the guidance of an ever-merciful God, may save us from destruction, and restore to us the bright hopes and prospects of the past.[16]

—Lee, writing amid the war-torn conditions of the postwar South, urging reconciliation between Northerners and Southerners

★ ★ ★

He bore it calmly and quietly, regretting what he called his awkwardness.[17]

—Capt. Henry Kyd Douglas, recalling Lee's reaction to a painful injury to his hands in 1862

★ ★ ★

$\mathcal{T}$each him he must deny himself.[18]

—Lee, responding to a Virginian mother's request for words of wisdom for her infant son

★ **SELF-CONTROL** ★

𝒯he gentleman does not needlessly and unnecessarily remind an offender of a wrong he may have committed against him. He cannot only forgive, he can forget.[19]

—From notes in Lee's handwriting found after his death

★ ★ ★

Only for a fleeting moment did he lose complete self-control. As he rode back from the McLean house [at Appomattox], his weeping men crowded around him, and as they assured him in broken voices of their confidence and love, his emotions momentarily overmastered him, and his wet cheeks told of the sorrow his words could not express.[20]

—Gen. John B. Gordon, recalling Lee
with his troops at Appomattox

Chapter 9

HUMILITY

Central to Lee's gentlemanly conduct was a clearly evident attitude of personal humility. It was reflected in his consistently polite manner. It was expressed in his habitual treatment of others. It embodied the Golden Rule—"Do unto others as you would have them do unto you."—and it also revealed what appears to have been Lee's genuinely humble spirit. It was said of Lee that he routinely treated dignitaries and common soldiers alike with the same gentle warmth and polite respect. Such humility was perhaps unexpected in one so acclaimed, and it especially endeared him to the common man. Lee's humility made him accessible, encouraged effective communications, encouraged loyalty—and left him respected in the North and revered in the South.[1]

★ **HUMILITY** ★

I tremble for my country, when I hear of confidence expressed in me. I know too well my weakness, and that our only hope is in God.[2]

—Lee, responding to public praise toward him

★ ★ ★

He assumed no airs of superior authority.[3]

—An officer from Virginia, recalling Lee in wartime

★ ★ ★

*O*ur success has not been as complete as we could desire, but God knows what is best for us.[4]

—Lee, reacting to his dramatic victory
in the 1862 Seven Days Campaign

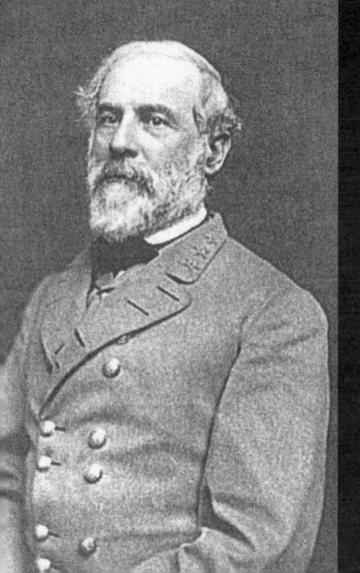

It is necessary we should be humbled and taught to be less boastful, less selfish and more devoted to right and justice.[5]

★ HUMILITY ★

I am willing to serve in any capacity to which the authorities may assign me.[6]

—Lee, expressing his submission to civilian authority

★ ★ ★

I would have much preferred your choice had fallen upon an abler man. Trusting in Almighty God, an approving conscience, and the aid of my fellow citizens, I devote myself to the service of my native state, in whose behalf alone will I ever again draw my sword.[7]

—Lee, officially accepting command of Virginia state troops in 1861

★ **HUMILITY** ★

It was in the afternoon of a winter's day and we were lounging in front of our tents, or rather huts, when President Davis and Gen. R. E. Lee came riding along the line. As soon as Lee was recognized the inevitable shout went up—a "Rebel yell." President Davis' hat was off, and he bowed right and left at the boys. Lee sat like a stone man on his horse, never turning his head to right or left. Apparently he heard not a sound. I was standing by our colonel, and, turning to me, the latter said: "Notice Lee's humility; he knows the cheering is for him, but he passes it all over to President Davis."[8]

—A Confederate soldier, recalling contact with Lee in the winter of 1864

★ **HUMILITY** ★

Could I have directed events, I should have chosen for the good of the country to be disabled in your stead.[9]

—*Letter from Lee to Stonewall Jackson in response to the news that Jackson had been wounded at the battle of Chancellorsville*

★ ★ ★

The general remedy for the want of success in a military commander is his removal. This is natural, and, in many instances, proper.... Everything, therefore, points to the advantages to be derived from a new commander, and I then anxiously urge the matter upon Your Excellency from my belief that a younger and abler man than myself can readily be obtained.[10]

—*Lee, tendering his resignation to President Davis following defeat at Gettysburg*

★ **HUMILITY** ★

But suppose, my dear friend, that I were to admit, with all their implications, the points which you present, where am I able to find that new commander who is to possess the greater ability which you believe to be required?[11]

—*Jefferson Davis, declining Lee's resignation*

★ ★ ★

The General is as unostentatious and unassuming in dress as he is in manners. He wears a colonel's coat (three stars without the wreath) . . . faded blue pantaloons, with top boots . . . and a high felt hat without adornments save a small cord around the crown.[12]

—*A description of Lee in the field by a Southern reporter*

★ **HUMILITY** ★

General Lee brought with him to Lexington the old iron-gray horse that he rode during the war. A few days after he had been there he rode up Main Street on his old war horse, and as he passed up the street the citizens cheered him. After passing the ordeal he hurried back to his home near the college, and never again appeared on the streets on horseback. He took his usual afternoon horse-back rides, but ever afterward he rode out back of the campus. . . . The demonstration was simply offensive to his innate modesty.[13]

—*A student at Washington College during Lee's tenure as president*

★ **HUMILITY** ★

My salary is as large as the college ought to pay.[14]
—*Response by Lee, who had increased enrollment at Washington College from 60 to 400 students, to a pay raise offered by the school's Board of Trustees*

★ ★ ★

Persons having business with his headquarters were treated like human beings, and courtesy, consideration, and even deference were shown to the humblest.[15]
—*Col. John S. Wise, who served on Lee's command staff*

★ **HUMILITY** ★

As far as anything like publicity, notoriety, or display, it was absolutely painful to him.[16]

—A contemporary of Lee during the peak of his popularity

★ ★ ★

I find it so hard to keep [this] one poor sinner's heart in the right way, that it seems presumptuous to try to help others.[17]

—Lee, agreeing to a request to counsel a mutual friend

★ ★ ★

He impressed me as being the most modest man I ever saw.[18]

—An elderly Southerner, who never forgot his teenaged introduction to Lee

Chapter 10

FAITH

Robert E. Lee was devout. The Judeo-Christian ethic was the dominant world view of nineteenth century America—especially among Southerners. Like so many of his countrymen, Lee professed a personal faith in Jesus Christ as Lord and Savior. This Biblical faith was the cornerstone of his heart and conduct. He officially requested prayer and fasting among his troops, supported the spiritual efforts of army chaplains, encouraged worship services and aided the distribution of Gospel tracts and Bibles.

The personal character that has endeared Lee to generations of admirers can be easily understood through a Biblical passage that was undoubtedly familiar to him: "But the fruit of the Spirit is love, joy, peace, long-suffering, gentleness, goodness, faith, meekness and temperance." Christ-centered obedience to such Biblical direction was the focus of Robert E. Lee's life.[1]

★ **FAITH** ★

$\mathcal{I}$ can only say that I am nothing but a poor sinner, trusting in Christ alone for salvation . . .[2]

—*Lee, sharing his personal theology with a group of army chaplains*

★ ★ ★

$\mathcal{N}$o day should be lived unless it was begun with a prayer of thankfulness and an intercession for guidance.[3]

—*An observation by Lee on daily planning and priorities*

> My trust is in the mercy and wisdom of a kind Providence.

★ **FAITH** ★

There are many things in the [Bible] which I may never be able to explain, but I accept it as the infallible word of God, and receive its teachings as inspired by the Holy Ghost.[5]

—Lee, on the inspiration and dependibility of Scripture

★ ★ ★

I am not concerned with results. God's will ought to be our aim, and I am quite contented that his designs should be accomplished and not mine.[6]

—Lee's response to a question about the likelihood of success

★ FAITH ★

$\mathcal{I}$ cannot express the anguish I feel at the death of my sweet Annie. To know that I shall never see her again on earth, that her place in our circle, which I always hoped one day to enjoy, is forever vacant, is agonizing in the extreme. But God, in this, as in all things, has mingled mercy with the blow, selecting that one best prepared to leave us. May you be able to join me in saying, "His will be done."[7]

—Lee, responding to the death of his daughter Annie, who was a devout Christian

★ **FAITH** ★

As soon as I order the troops forward into battle, I lay the fate of my army in the hand of God.[8]

—From a letter by Lee to a foreign military observer inquiring about strategy

★ ★ ★

I cannot hope that Heaven will prosper our cause when we are violating its laws. I shall, therefore, carry on the war in Pennsylvania without offending the sanctions of a high civilization and of Christianity.[9]

—Lee's response to suggestions that his army retaliate against the citizens of Pennsylvania for destruction inflicted on Virginia's residents by Northern troops

★ **FAITH** ★

$\mathcal{B}$ut what a cruel thing is war; to separate and destroy families and friends, and mar the purest joys and happiness God has granted us in this world; to fill our hearts with hatred instead of love for our neighbours, and to devastate the fair face of this beautiful world![10]

—Excerpt from a letter by Lee to his wife soon after the 1862 battle of Fredericksburg

★ ★ ★

$\mathcal{M}$ay God enable me to perform my duty and not suffer me to be tempted beyond my strength.[11]

—Lee, writing to a colleague in the opening days of war

★ **FAITH** ★

I can never forget my first interview and conversation with General Lee on religious matters. It was in February, 1864, while our army was resting along the Rapidan. Rev. B.T. Lacy and myself went, as a committee of our Chaplain's Association, to consult him in reference to the better observance of the Sabbath. . . . The cordial greeting which he gave us, the marked courtesy and respect with which he listened to what we had to say . . . soon put us at our ease. But as we presently began to answer his questions concerning the spiritual interests of the army and to tell of that great revival which was then extending through the camps and bringing thousands of our noble men to Christ, we saw his eye brighten and his whole countenance glow with pleasure; and as, in his simple, feeling words, he expressed his delight, we forgot the great warrior, and only remembered that we were communing with an humble, earnest Christian.[12]

—*Army Chaplain J. William Jones*

★ **FAITH** ★

We must be resigned to necessity and commit ourselves in adversity to the will of a merciful God as cheerfully as in posterity.[13]
 —*From a letter by Lee responding to reports of Southern suffering*

★ ★ ★

The sunshine and in storm, in victory and in defeat, his heart turned to God.[14]
 —*Gen. John B. Gordon, CSA*

★ ★ ★

I believe I may say, looking into my own heart, and speaking as in the presence of God, that I have never known one moment of bitterness or resentment.[15]
 —*Response by Lee to a question about his feelings toward the North*

★ FAITH ★

We failed, but in the good providence of God apparent failure often proves a blessing.[16]

—*Lee, responding to a comment on the defeat of the South*

★ ★ ★

Be true, kind and generous, and pray earnestly to God to enable you to keep His commandments and walk in the same all the days of your life.[17]

—*Advice for life from a letter by Lee to his son, Robert E. Lee, Jr.*

LEE'S LETTER TO GEN. WINFIELD SCOTT

Lt. Gen. Winfield Scott
Commanding United States Army
Arlington, Va., April 20, 1861

General: Since my interview with you on the 18th instant, I have felt that I ought not longer to retain my commission in the army. I therefore tender my resignation, which I request you will recommend for acceptance. It would have been presented at once but for the struggle if has caused me to separate myself from a service to which I have devoted the best years of my life, and all the ability I possessed.

During the whole of that time—more than a quarter of a century—I have experienced nothing but kindness from my superiors, and the most cordial friendship from my comrades. To no one, General, have I been as much indebted as to yourself, for uniform kindness and consideration, and it has always been my ardent desire to merit your approbation. I shall carry to the grave the most grateful recollections of your kind consideration, and your name and fame will always be dear to me.

Save in defence of my native State, I never desire again to draw my sword. Be pleased to accept my most earnest wishes for the continuance of your happiness and prosperity, and believe me, most truly yours,

R. E. Lee

Lee's Orders for the Invasion of Pennsylvania

General Orders No. 73
Hdqtrs, Army of Northern Virginia
Chambersburg, Pa., June 27, 1863

The commanding general has observed with marked satisfaction the conduct of the troops on the march, and confidently anticipates results commensurate with the high spirit they have manifested.

No troops could have displayed greater fortitude or better performed the arduous marches of the past ten days.

Their conduct in other respects has, with few exceptions, been in keeping with their character as soldiers, and entitles them to approbation and praise.

There have, however, been instances of forgetfulness, on the part of some, that they have in keeping the yet unsullied reputation of the army, and that the duties exacted of us by civilization and Christianity are not less obligatory in the country of the enemy than in our own.

Lee's Orders for the Invasion of Pennsylvania

The commanding general considers no greater disgrace could befall the army, and through it our whole people, than the perpetration of the barbarous outrages upon the unarmed and defenseless and the wanton destruction of private property, that have marked the course of the enemy in our own country.

Such proceedings not only degrade the perpetrators and all connected with them, but are subversive of the discipline and efficiency of the army, and destructive of the ends of our present movement.

It must be remembered that we make war only upon armed men, and that we cannot take vengeance for the wrongs our people have suffered without lowering ourselves in the eyes of all whose abhorrence has been excited by the atrocities of our enemies, and offending against Him to whom vengeance belongeth, without whose favor and support our efforts must all prove in vain.

The commanding general therefore earnestly exhorts the troops to abstain with most scrupulous care from unnecessary or wanton injury to private property, and he enjoins upon all officers to arrest and bring to summary punishment all who shall in any way offend against the orders on this subject.

R. E. Lee, General

LEE'S ORDER FOR WORSHIP

General Orders No. 83.
Head-quarters, A. N. Va., August 13, 1863.

The President of the Confederate States has, in the name of the people, appointed the 21st day of August as a day of fasting, humiliation and prayer. A strict observance of the day is enjoined upon the officers and soldiers of this army. All military duties, except such as are absolutely necessary, will be suspended. The commanding officers of brigades and regiments are requested to cause divine service, suitable to the occasion, to be performed in their respective commands. Soldiers! We have sinned against Almighty God. We have forgotten His signal mercies, and have cultivated a revengeful, haughty, and boastful spirit. We have not remembered that the defenders of a just cause should be pure in His eyes; that 'our times are in His hands;' and we have relied too much on our own arms for the achievement of our independence. God is our only refuge and our strength. Let us humble ourselves before Him. Let us confess our many sins, and beseech Him to give us a higher courage, a purer patriotism and more determined will; that He will convert the hearts of our enemies; that He will hasten the time when war, with its sorrows and sufferings, shall cease, and that He will give us a name and place among the nations of the earth.

R. E. Lee, General

Lee's Farewell Address

General Orders No. 9
Headquarters Army of Northern Virginia,
Appomattox Courthouse, April 10, 1865.

After four years' arduous service, marked by unsurpassed courage and fortitude, the Army of Northern Virginia has been compelled to yield to overwhelming numbers and resources.

I need not tell the survivors of so many hard fought battles who have remained steadfast to the last, that I have consented to this result from no distrust of them, but feeling that valor and devotion could accomplish nothing that could compensate for the loss which would have attended the continuation of the contest, I have determined to avoid the useless sacrifice of those whose past services have endeared them to their countrymen. You will take with you the satisfaction that proceeds from the consciousness of duty faithfully performed, and I earnestly pray that a merciful God may extend to you His blessing and protection. With an increasing admiration of your constancy and devotion to your country, and a

★ LEE'S FAREWELL ADDRESS ★

grateful remembrance of your kind and generous consideration of myself, I bid you an affectionate farewell.

Robert E. Lee, General

NOTES

LEE BIOGRAPHY

Dictionary of American Biography, edited by Allen Johnson and Dumas Malone (New York: Charles Scribner's Sons, 1928–1936), 10:120–129.

Douglas Southall Freeman, *R. E. Lee: A Biography* (New York: Charles Scribner's Sons, 1934), 1:463–467.

Encyclopedia of the Confederacy, edited by Richard N. Current (New York: Simon & Schuster, 1993), 2:916–920.

Historical Times Illustrated Encyclopedia of the Civil War, edited by Patricia Faust (New York: Harper & Row, 1986), 429–431.

Douglas Southall Freeman, *Lee's Lieutenants: A Study in Command* (New York: Charles Scribner's Sons, 1942), 3:740–752.

Ernest B. Furgurson, "Rethinking Robert E. Lee," *Washingtonian* (April 2000), 74–77, 124–127.

CHAPTER 1: DUTY

1. *Dictionary of American Biography,* 10:120–129; Armistead Long, *Memoirs of Robert E. Lee* (New York: J. M. Stoddard & Co., 1886), 465; Furgurson, "Rethinking Robert E. Lee," 74–77, 124–127.

2. Long, *Memoirs of Robert E. Lee,* 405.

3. William J. Jones, *Personal Reminiscences, Anedotes and Letters of General Lee* (New York: D. Appleton, 1875), 145.

4. Freeman, *R. E. Lee,* 1:475.

5. Freeman, *R. E. Lee,* 1:423.

6. Furguson, "Rethinking Robert E. Lee," 77.

7. Alexander Stephens, *A Constitutional View of the War Between the States* (Philadelphia: National Publishing Co., 1870), 2:386–387.
8. Jones, *Reminiscences of General Lee*, 142.
9. John Purifoy, "General Lee's Letters," *Confederate Veteran* 34, (March 1926), 101.
10. Freeman, *R. E. Lee*, 2:347.
11. Henry A. White, *Robert E. Lee and the Southern Confederacy* (New York, n.p., 1897), 173.
12. Jones, *Reminiscences of General Lee*, 144.
13. D. B. Strouse, "Gen. R. E. Lee to a Careless Student," *Confederate Veteran* 16 (September 1908), 455–456.
14. Robert E. Lee Jr., *Recollections and Letters of General Robert E. Lee* (Garden City, N.Y.: Garden City Publishing Co., 1904), 170.
15. Freeman, *R. E. Lee*, 4:278.
16. Freeman, *R. E. Lee*, 1:362.
17. John Hampden Chamberlayne, "Address on the Character of Robert E. Lee," *Southern Historical Society Papers*, 3:31.

CHAPTER 2: LEADERSHIP

1. Freeman, *R. E. Lee*, 4:185, 187; Long, *Memoirs of Robert E. Lee*, 435; John Bell Hood, *Advance and Retreat* (New Orleans: Hood Orphan Memorial Fund, 1880), 53.
2. John W. Daniel, "Unveiling of Valentine's Recumbent Figure of Lee," *Southern Historical Society Papers*, 11:379.

★ NOTES ★

3. Hood, *Advance and Retreat*, 53.
4. Jones, *Reminiscences of General Lee*, 381.
5. Freeman, *R. E. Lee*, 1:410.
6. White, *Robert E. Lee and the Southern Confederacy*, 71.
7. Frank M. Mixson, *Reminiscences of a Private* (Columbia, S.C.: State Printing Co., 1910), 65.
8. James Longstreet, *From Manassas to Appomattox: Memoirs of the Civil War in America* (Secaucus, N.J.: Blue and Grey Press, 1984), 158.
9. Joel Cook, *The Siege of Richmond* (Philadephia: George W. Childs, 1862), 246–247.
10. Long, *Memoirs of Robert E. Lee*, 465.
11. Chamberlayne, "Character of Lee," 198.
12. Edward Porter Alexander, *Military Memoirs of a Confederate* (New York: Charles Scribner's Sons, 1910), 110–111.
13. Richard Taylor, *Deconstruction and Reconstruction: Personal Experiences in the Late War* (New York: D. Appleton and Company, 1879–96).
14. *The War of the Rebellion: A Compilation of the Official Records of the Union and Confederate Armies* (Washington, D.C.: U.S. Government Printing Office, 1880–1901), series 1, vol. 12, part 3, 925–926.
15. T. C. DeLeon, *Four Years in Rebel Capitals* (Mobile: The Gossip Printing Co., 1890), 404.
16. *Mary Chestnut's Civil War*, edited by C. Vann Woodward (New Haven: Yale University Press, 1981), 388.
17. *New York Herald*, 30 January 1865.

18. Freeman, *R. E. Lee*, 4:218.
19. Jones, *Reminiscences of General Lee*, 244.
20. Freeman, *R. E. Lee*, 3:331.
21. John B. Gordon, *Reminiscences of the Civil War* (New York: Charles Scribner's Sons, 1903), 232.
22. John H. Worsham, *One of Jackson's Foot Cavalry* (New York: Neale Publishing Co., 1912), 188.

CHAPTER 3: INTEGRITY

1. *Dictionary of American Biography* 10:120–129; DeLeon, *Four Years in Rebel Capitals*, 404.
2. *Personal Memoirs of Ulysses S. Grant* (New York: Charles L. Webster Co, 1894), 634.
3. J. William Jones, "A Brief Sketch of Gen. R. E. Lee," *Confederate Veteran* 1 (December 1893), 357.
4. Lee, *Recollections of General Lee*, 282.
5. Jones, *Reminiscences of General Lee*, 174–175.
6. Jones, *Reminiscences of General Lee*, 232.
7. Freeman, *R. E. Lee*, 1:92.
8. Furguson, "Rethinking Robert E. Lee," 77.
9. Freeman, *R. E. Lee*, 4:401.
10. *Official Records*, series 1, vol. 21, 1067.
11. Long, *Memoirs of Robert E. Lee*, 464.

★ **NOTES** ★

12. *Official Records*, series 1, vol.19, part 2, 722.
13. Long, *Memoirs of Robert E. Lee*, 486.
14. Jacob Hoke, *The Great Invasion of 1863*, (New York: W. J. Shey, 1888), 198.
15. William C. Jones, *The Life and Letters of Lee, Soldier and Man* (Washington: n.p., 1906), 118–119.
16. Jones, "Sketch of Lee," 357.
17. Long, *Memoirs of Robert E. Lee*, 643.
18. Gordon, *Reminiscences of the Civil War*, 308–309.

CHAPTER 4: DIGNITY

1. *Dictionary of American Biography* 10:120–129; *Encyclopedia of the Confederacy* 2:916–920; Chamberlayne, "Character of Lee," 28–37; Daniel, "Unveiling of Valentine's Figure of Lee," 372–373.
2. Rod Gragg, *The Illustrated Confederate Reader* (New York: Harper & Row, 1989), 223.
3. Jones, *Reminiscences of General Lee*, 235.
4. Ibid.
5. "Comment on General Lee at the North," *Confederate Veteran* 14 (October 1906), 466.
6. Worsham, *One of Jackson's Foot Cavalry*, 299.
7. "Comment on General Lee," 466.
8. William E. Hatcher, *Along the Trail of the Friendly Years* (New York: n.p., 1910), 118–119.

NOTES

9. Theodore Lyman, *Meade's Headquarters, 1863–1865* (Boston: Atlantic Monthly Press, 1922), 360–361.
10. *The Fremantle Diary*, edited by Walter Lord (Boston: Little, Brown and Co., 1954), 197–198.
11. Jones, *Reminiscences of General Lee*, 147.
12. Hatcher, *Along the Trail of Friendly Years*, 118–119.
13. Stephens, *Constitutional View of the War Between the States*, 2:384.
14. Worsham, *One of Jackson's Foot Cavalry*, 299.
15. *The Fremantle Diary*, 197.

CHAPTER 5: KINDNESS

1. G. Moxley Sorrel, *Recollections of a Confederate Staff Officer* (Jackson, Tenn.: McCowat-Mercer Press, 1958), 173; Daniel, "Unveiling of Valentine's Figure of Lee," 377; Jones, *Reminiscences of General Lee*, 319.
2. John B. Colvar, "A Boy's Observations of Gen. Lee," *Confederate Veteran* 1 (September 1893), 265.
3. William Stanley Hoole, *Lawley Covers the Confederacy* (Tuscaloosa: Confederate Publishing Co., 1964), 31.
4. Daniel, "Unveiling of Valentine's Figure of Lee," 378.
5. Jones, *Reminiscences of General Lee*, 196.
6. Jones, *Reminiscences of General Lee*, 196.
7. Jones, *Reminiscences of General Lee*, 197.
8. Thomas Lafayette Rosser, *The Cavalry, A. N. V.* (Baltimore: n.p., 1889), 239.

9. Worsham, *One of Jackson's Foot Cavalry,* 16.
10. Walter B. Barker, "Two Anecdotes of General Lee," *Southern Historical Society Papers* 12:329.
11. Theodore Hartman, "Some Incidents of Army Life," *Confederate Veteran* 30 (February 1922), 45.
12. J. William Jones, "Reminiscences of the Army of Northern Virginia," *Southern Historical Society Papers,* 9:562.
13. Long, *Memoirs of Robert E. Lee,* 306.
14. Long, *Memoirs of Robert E. Lee,* 435.
15. Daniel, "Unveiling of Valentine's Figure of Lee," 381.
16. Royal W. Figg, *"Where Only Men Dare to Go!"* (Richmond: Whittet & Shepperson, 1885), 204.
17. Freeman, *R. E. Lee,* 4:411.

CHAPTER 6: RESPONSIBILITY

1. *Dictionary of American Biography* 10:120–129.; Freeman, *R. E. Lee,* 2:86.
2. Freeman, *R. E. Lee,* 2:86.
3. *Lee's Aide-de-Camp: The Papers of Colonel Charles Marshall,* edited by Frederick Maurice (Boston: Little & Brown, Co., 1927), 61.
4. T. C. Morton, "Anecdotes of General Robert E. Lee," *Southern Historical Society Papers* 2:519.
5. Robert A. Bright,"Pickett's Change at Gettysburg," *Southern Historical Society Papers* 31:234.
6. Long, *Memoirs of Robert E. Lee,* 388.

★ NOTES ★

7. Freeman, *R. E. Lee*, 1:247.
8. Jones, *Reminiscences of General Lee*, 369.
9. Long, *Memoirs of Robert E. Lee*, 464.
10. Long, *Memoirs of Robert E. Lee*, 643.
11. *Fremantle Diary*, 214–215.
12. Freeman, *R. E. Lee*, 4:278.
13. *Official Records*, series 1, vol. 19, part 2, 722.
14. Jones, *Reminiscences of General Lee*, 144.
15. Jones, *Reminiscences of General Lee*, 145.
16. Gordon, *Reminiscences of the Civil War*, 132.
17. Paul C. Nagel, *The Lees of Virginia: Seven Generations of an American Family* (New York: Oxford University Press, 1990), 256.
18. Nagel, *Lees of Virginia*, 251.
19. Freeman, *R. E. Lee*, 1:361–362.

CHAPTER 7: COURAGE

1. *Dictionary of American Biography* 10:120–129; Long, *Memoirs of Robert E. Lee*, 389.
2. Nancy and Dwight Anderson, *The Generals* (New York: Wings Books, 1987), 385–386.
3. Freeman, *R. E. Lee*, 1:248.
4. Long, *Memoirs of Robert E. Lee*, 464.
5. Purifoy, "General Lee's Letters," 101.

6. John S. Mosby, *The Memoirs of Colonel John S. Mosby* (Boston: Little, Brown Co., 1917), 374.
7. Charles Venable, "General Lee to the Rear," *Southern Historical Society Papers* 8:108–109.
8. J. B. Minor, "Gen. Robert E. Lee Under Fire," *Confederate Veteran* 27 (July 1909), 328.
9. John Esten Cooke, *A Life of Robert E. Lee* (New York: G. W. Dillingham, 1899), 404.
10. Heros von Borcke, *Memoirs of the Confederate War for Independence* (Philadelphia: J. P. Lippincott, 1867), 239.
11. Long, *Memoirs of Robert E. Lee*, 389.
12. Walter H. Taylor, *Four Years With General Lee* (New York: D. Appleton Co., 1877), 196–197.
13. Sorrel, *Confederate Staff Officer*, 73.
14. Purifoy, "General Lee's Letters," 102.
15. Alexander, *Fighting for the Confederacy*, 532.
16. Long, *Memoirs of R. E. Lee*, 421.

CHAPTER 8: SELF-CONTROL

1. *Dictionary of American Biography* 10: 120–129; Daniel, "Unveiling of Valentine's Figure of Lee," 372–373; Freeman, *R. E. Lee*, 3:250.
2. Jones, *Reminiscences of General Lee*, 170.
3. John Lamp, "Address of the Hon. John Lamp at New Market," *Southern Historical Society Papers* 38:304.
4. Lee, *Recollections of General Lee*, 281.

★ NOTES ★

5. Nagle, *Lees of Virginia,* 256.
6. Jones, *Reminiscences of General Lee,* 169.
7. Jones, *Reminiscences of General Lee,* 171–172.
8. Leigh Robinson, "Unpublished Letters of General Lee," *Confederate Veteran* 31 (August 1923), 287.
9. Long, *Memoirs of Robert E. Lee,* 464.
10. Freeman, *R. E. Lee,* 1:477.
11. Hood, *Advance and Retreat,* 51.
12. Taylor, *Four Years with General Lee,* 77.
13. Channing Smith, "The Last Time I Saw General Lee," *Confederate Veteran* 35 (September 1927), 327.
14. Jones, *Reminiscences of General Lee,* 204.
15. Jones, *Reminiscences of General Lee,* 217.
16. Jones, *Reminiscences of General Lee,* 206.
17. Henry Kyd Douglas, *I Rode With Stonewall* (Chapel Hill: University of North Carolina Press, 1940), 143.
18. Freeman, *R. E. Lee,* 4:505.
19. Jones, *Reminiscences of General Lee,* 163.
20. Gordon, *Reminiscences of the Civil War,* 460.

CHAPTER 9: HUMILITY

1. Colvar, "A Boy's Observations of Gen. Lee," 265; Luke 6:31 (KJV); Giles B. Cooke, "Word Picture of General Lee," *Confederate Veteran* 34 (September 1926), 355.

★ NOTES ★

2. Freeman, *R. E. Lee*, 2:440.
3. Cooke, "Word Picture of General Lee," 355.
4. Gordon, *Reminiscences of the Civil War*, 232.
5. Lee, *Recollections of General Lee*, 64.
6. Jones, *Reminiscences of General Lee*, 241–242.
7. Stephens, *Constitutional View of the War Between the States*, 2:384.
8. James B. Hodgkin, "Home Life of Gen. R. E. Lee's Family," *Confederate Veteran* 15 (September 1907), 399.
9. *Official Records*, series 1, vol. 25, part 2, 769.
10. *Official Records*, series 1, vol. 51, part 2, 752.
11. *Official Records*, series 1, vol. 29, part 2, 640.
12. *New York Herald*, 30 January 1865.
13. Colvar, "A Boy's Observations of Gen. Lee," 265.
14. Jones, *Reminiscences of General Lee*, 177.
15. Cooke, "Word Picture of General Lee," 355.
16. Colvar, "A Boy's Observations of Gen. Lee," 265.
17. Jones, *Life and Letters of Robert E. Lee*, 156.
18. Colvar, "A Boy's Observations of Gen. Lee," 265.

CHAPTER 10: FAITH

1. J. William Jones, *Christ in the Camp: Religion in the Confederate Army* (Atlanta: Martin & Hoyt Co., 1904), 50–53; Freeman, *R. E. Lee*, 3:241; Galations 5:22–23 (KJV).

★ NOTES ★

2. Jones, *Christ in the Camp*, 50.
3. Freeman, *R. E. Lee*, 4:380.
4. Freeman, *R. E. Lee*, 1:350.
5. Freeman, *R. E. Lee*, 4:298.
6. Jones, *Reminiscences of General Lee*, 143.
7. Lee, *Recollections of General Lee*, 79–80.
8. Freeman, *R. E. Lee*, 2:347.
9. Isaac R. Trimble, "The Battle and Campaign of Gettysburg," *Southern Historical Society Papers*, 26:119.
10. Lee, *Recollections of General Lee*, 89.
11. Freeman, *R. E. Lee*, 1:476.
12. Jones, *Christ in the Camp*, 50.
13. Freeman, *R. E. Lee*, 4:329.
14. Flood, *Lee: The Last Years*, 56.
15. Gordon, *Reminiscences of the Civil War*, 232.
16. Jones, *Reminiscences of General Lee*, 274.
17. Lee, *Recollections of General Lee*, 16.

Bibliography

Alexander, Edward Porter. *Military Memoirs of a Confederate.* New York: Charles Scribner's Sons, 1910.

Anderson, Nancy and Dwight. *The Generals.* New York: Wings Books, 1987.

Barker, Walter B. "Two Anecdotes of General Lee." *Southern Historical Society Papers* 12.

Borcke, Heros von. *Memoirs of the Confederate War for Independence.* Philadelphia: Lippincott Co., 1867.

Bright, Robert A. "Pickett's Charge at Gettysburg," *Southern Historical Society Papers* 31.

Chamberlayne, John Hampden. "Address on the Character of General R. E. Lee." *Southern Historical Society Papers* 3.

Colvar, John B. "A Boy's Observations of Gen. Lee." *Confederate Veteran* 1 (September 1893).

"Comment on General Lee at the North." *Confederate Veteran* 14 (October 1906).

Cook, Joel. *The Siege of Richmond.* Philadelphia: *George W. Childs,* 1862.

Cooke, Giles B. "Word Picture of General Lee." *Confederate Veteran* 34 (September 1926).

Cooke, John Esten. A Life of Robert E. Lee. New York: G. W. Dillingham Co., 1899.

Daniel, John W. "Unveiling of Valentine's Recumbent Figure of Lee." *Southern Historical Society Papers* 11.

DeLeon, T. C. Four Years in Rebel Capitals. Mobile: The Gossip Printing Co., 1890.

Dictionary of American Biography. Edited by Allen Johnson and Dumas Malone. New York: Charles Scribner's Sons, 1928–1936.

Douglas, Henry Kyd. *I Rode With Stonewall.* Chapel Hill: University of North Carolina Press, 1940.

Encyclopedia of the Confederacy. Edited by Richard N. Current. New York: Simon & Schuster, 1993.

Figg, Royal W. *Where Only Men Dare to Go!* Richmond: Whittet & Shepperson, 1885.

Fighting for the Confederacy: The Personal Recollections of General Edward Porter Alexander. Edited by Gary W. Gallagher. Chapel Hill: University of North Carolina Press, 1984.

★ **BIBLIOGRAPHY** ★

Freeman, Douglas Southall. *Lee's Lieutenants: A Study in Command.* New York: Charles Scribner's Sons, 1942.

Freeman, Douglas Southall. *R. E. Lee: A Biography.* New York: Charles Scribner's Sons, 1934.

The Fremantle Diary. Edited by Walter Lord. Boston: Little, Brown and Co., 1954.

Flood, Charles Bracelen. *Lee: The Last Years.* Boston: Houghton Mifflin Co., 1981.

Furgurson, Ernest B. "Rethinking Robert E. Lee." *The Washingtonian* (April 2000).

Gordon, John B. *Reminiscence of the Civil War.* New York: Neale Publishing Co., 1912.

Gragg, Rod. *The Illustrated Confederate Reader.* New York: Harper & Row, 1989.

Hartman, Theodore. "Some Incidents of Army Life." *Confederate Veteran* 30 (February 1922).

Hatcher, William E. *Along the Trail of the Friendly Years.* New York: n.p., 1910.

Historical Times Illustrated Encyclopedia of the Civil War. Edited by Patricia Faust. New York: Harper & Row, 1986.

Hodgkin, James B. "Home Life of Gen. R. E. Lee's Family." *Confederate Veteran* 15 (September 1907).

Hoke, Jacob. *The Great Invasion of 1863.* Dayton, Ohio: W. J. Shey, 1888.

Hoole, William Stanley. *Lawley Covers the Confederacy.* Tuscaloosa: Confederate Publishing Company, 1964.

Hood, John Bell. *Advance and Retreat.* New Orleans: Hood Orphan Memorial Fund, 1880.

Johnston, David E. *The Story of a Confederate Boy in the Civil War.* Portland: n.p., 1914.

Jones, J. William. "A Brief Sketch of Gen. R. E. Lee." *Confederate Veteran* 1. (December 1893).

Jones, J. William. *Christ in the Camp: Religion in the Confederate Army.* Atlanta: Martin & Hoyt Co., 1904.

Jones, J. William. *Life and Letters of Robert Edward Lee: Soldier and Man.* Washington, n.p., 1906.

★ BIBLIOGRAPHY ★

Jones, J. William. *Personal Reminiscences, Anecdotes and Letters of Gen. Robert E. Lee.* New York: D. Appleton, 1875.

Jones, J. William. "Reminiscences of the Army of Northern Virginia." *Southern Historical Society Papers* 9:562.

Lamp, John. "Address of the Hon. John Lamp at New Market." *Southern Historical Society Papers* 38.

Lee, Fitzhugh. *General Lee.* New York: D. Appleton Co., 1901.

Lee, Robert E. Jr. *Recollections and Letters of General Robert E. Lee.* Garden City, New York: Garden City Publishing Co., 1904.

Lee's Aide-de-Camp: The Papers of Colonel Charles Marshall. Edited by Frederick Maurice. Boston: Little, Brown and Company, 1927.

Long, Armistead L. *Memoirs of Robert E. Lee.* New York: J. M. Stoddart & Co., 1886.

Longstreet, James. *From Manassas to Appomattox: Memiors of the Civil War in America.* Secaucus, N. J.: Blue and Gray Press, 1984.

Lyman, Theodore. *Meade's Headquarters, 1863–1865.* Boston: The Atlantic Monthly Press, 1922.

Mary Chestnut's Civil War. Edited by C. Vann Woodward. New Haven: Yale University Press, 1981.

The Memoirs of Colonel John S. Mosby. Boston: Little, Brown Co., 1917.

Minor, J. B. "Gen. Robert E. Lee Under Fire." *Confederate Veteran* 27 July 1909.

Mixson, Frank M. *Reminiscences of a Private.* Columbia, S.C.: State Printing Co., 1910.

Morton, T. C. "Anecdotes of General Robert E. Lee." *Southern Historical Society Papers* 2.

Nagel, Paul C. *The Lees of Virginia: Seven Generations of an American Family.* New York: Oxford University Press, 1990.

New York Herald.

New York Times.

Personal Memoirs of Ulysses S. Grant. New York: Charles L. Webster & Co., 1894.

Purifoy, John. "General Lee's Letters," *Confederate Veteran* 34 (March 1926).

Robertson, James I. *Stonewall Jackson: the Man, the Soldier, the Legend.* New York: MacMillan Publishing USA, 1997.

Robinson, Leigh. "Unpublished Letters of General Lee." *Confederate Veteran* 31 (August 1923).

Rosser, Thomas Lafayette. *The Cavalry, A. N. V.* Baltimore: n.p., 1889.

"Senator Ben Hill Tribute," *Confederate Veteran* 1 (December 1893).

Smith, Channing. "The Last Time I Saw General Lee." *Confederate Veteran* 35.

Sorrel, G. Moxley. *Recollections of a Confederate Staff Officer.* Jackson, Tennessee: McCowat-Mercer Press, 1958.

Stephens, Alexander H. *A Constitutional View of the War Between the States.* Philadelphia: National Publishing Co., 1870.

Strouse, D. B., "Gen. R. E. Lee to a Careless Student." *Confederate Veteran* 16 (September 1908).

Taylor, Richard. *Destruction and Reconstruction: Personal Experiences in the Late War.* New York: D. Appleton and Company, 1879.

Taylor, Walter H. *Four Years With General Lee.* New York: D. Appleton Co., 1877.

Trimble, Isaac R. "The Battle and Campaign of Gettysburg." *Southern Historical Society Papers* 26.

Venable, Charles. "General Lee the Rear." *Southern Historical Society Papers* 8.

War of the Rebellion: The Official Records of the Union and Confederate Armies. Washington: U.S. Government Printing Office, 1887.

White, Henry A. *Robert E. Lee and the Southern Confederacy.* New York: n.p., 1897.

Worsham, John H. *One of Jackson's Foot Cavalry.* New York: Neale Publishing Company, 1912.